Clean Eating: Anti-Inflammatory Diet Breakfast Recipes

50+ Anti-Inflammation Diet & Clean Eating Recipes to Reduce Pain and Restore Health (2nd Edition)

ISBN 978-1-80095-021-4

Copyright ©Kira Novac 2016

www.amazon.com/author/kira-novac

All rights reserved. No part of this publication may be reproduced, stored in a retrieval system, or transmitted, in any form or by any means, electronic, mechanical, photocopying, recording or otherwise, without the prior written permission of the author and the publishers.

The scanning, uploading, and distribution of this book via the Internet, or via any other means, without the permission of the author is illegal and punishable by law. Please purchase only authorized electronic editions, and do not participate in or encourage electronic piracy of copyrighted materials.

All information in this book has been carefully researched and checked for factual accuracy. However, the author and publishers make no warranty, expressed or implied, that the information contained herein is appropriate for every individual, situation or purpose, and assume no responsibility for errors or omission. The reader assumes the risk and full responsibility for all actions, and the author will not be held liable for any loss or damage, whether consequential, incidental, and special or otherwise, that may result from the information presented in this publication.

A physician has not written the information in this book. Before making any serious dietary changes, I advise you to consult with your physician first.

Table of contents

Introduction 1
PART I Anti-Inflammatory Smoothies 5
   Cucumber Kiwi Green Smoothie 6
   Tropical Pineapple Kiwi Smoothie 8
   Sweet Cherry and Chia Smoothie 9
   Spinach Green Tea Smoothie... 10
   Fruity and Spicy Smoothie 12
   Leafy Green Apple Smoothie for Optimal Health 14
   Alkalizing Avocado Coconut Smoothie 15
   Blueberry Watermelon Smoothie 16
   Ginger Berry Green Smoothie 18
   Banana, Honey and Ginger Smoothie 19
   Dreamy Yummy Orange Cream Smoothie 20
   Blueberry Green Tea Smoothie 21
   Peachy Keen Smoothie 22
   Alkalizing Mango Apricot Smoothie 24
   Cucumber Melon Smoothie 25
   Triple Berry Vanilla Smoothie 26
   Tropical Mango Coconut Smoothie 27
   Blueberry Pomegranate Smoothie 29
   Pineapple and Greens Smoothie 30
PART II Energy-Boosting Breakfast Recipes 31
   Mushroom, Spinach and Onion Frittata..................................32
   Sausage and Onion Omelet 34
   Coconut Flour Zucchini Muffins 36
   Skillet Eggs with Spinach 38

Eggs Baked in Avocado 40

Herbed Onion Omelet 42

Greek-Style Spinach Frittata 44

Apple Cinnamon Muffins 46

Onion Ring Baked Eggs 48

Spicy Sausage and Onion Frittata 49

Paleo Blueberry Cinnamon Muffins 51

Mushroom and Onion Omelet 53

Paleo Spiced Pumpkin Muffins 55

PART III Easy Breakfast Wraps and Crepes 57

Gluten-Free Matcha Crepes 58

Paleo-Friendly Coconut Wraps 60

Homemade Brown Rice Wraps 62

Avocado Egg Salad Breakfast Wrap 64

Onion, Egg and Spinach Breakfast Wrap 66

Egg, Ham and Onion Breakfast Wrap 68

Paleo-Friendly Tapioca Flour Crepes 70

Easy Rice Flour Crepes 72

Paleo Coconut Flour Crepes 74

Banana and Hemp Protein Crepes 76

Almond Butter and Banana-Filled Crepes 78

Sweet Cinnamon Apple Crepes 80

Chocolate Hazelnut Crepes 81

Pineapple Coconut Crepes 83

PART IV Anti-Inflammatory Bakes and Bowls 84

Sausage and Egg Breakfast Bake 85

Cinnamon Spiced Quinoa Bowl 87

Simply Paleo Porridge 88
Mixed Veggie Baked Quiche 89
Honey Walnut Quinoa Bowl 91
Amaranth Coconut Porridge 93
Spinach, Mushroom and Sweet Potato Breakfast Bake 94
Cinnamon Pumpkin Porridge 96
Apple Cinnamon Quinoa Bowl...98
Veggies and Eggs Breakfast Bake..100
Buckwheat and Banana Porridge 102
Broccoli Sausage Baked Quiche 104
Honey Almond Paleo Porridge 106

Conclusion...109
To post an honest review 111
Recommended Reading..114

Free Complimentary Recipe eBook

Thank you so much for taking an interest in my work!

As a thank you, I would love to offer you a free complimentary recipe eBook to help you achieve vibrant health. It will teach you how to prepare amazingly tasty and healthy gluten-free treats so that you never feel deprived or bored again!

As a special bonus, you will be able to receive all my future books (kindle format) for free or only $0.99.

Download your free recipe eBook here:

http://bit.ly/gluten-free-desserts-book

GLUTEN-FREE, GUILT-FREE AND STRESS-FREE!

Irresistible Gluten-Free Snacks and Treats for Weight Loss and...

(PALEO AND VEGAN OPTIONS)

KIRA NOVAC

FREE GIFT — LIMITED OFFER

Introduction

Tasty and Healthy Anti-Inflammatory Diet Breakfast Recipes

Inflammation is your body's natural process for self-preservation. When you sustain an injury, the site surrounding the injury becomes inflamed (swollen) – this draws blood to the area to help start the healing process. When inflammation becomes chronic, however, it has the potential to do some serious damage to your body. Chronic inflammation has been linked to a number of serious diseases and conditions including asthma, rheumatoid arthritis, ulcerative colitis, and Crohn's disease. This type of inflammation can last for months, or even years, doing slow but steady damage to your body and to your immune system.

What can you do about chronic inflammation other than fill your body with prescription drugs? You can make simple changes to your diet to help reduce inflammation and to provide relief from a wide variety of inflammatory diseases. The anti-inflammatory diet is actually very simple to follow – there are no complicated rules to learn or crazy restrictions to follow. What you need to do is increase your consumption of fresh and nutritious foods like fruits, vegetables, whole grains, and healthy fats. By making positive changes to your diet you can reduce inflammation and improve your overall health. Why wouldn't you give it a try?

In order to follow the anti-inflammatory diet, you should cut back on your consumption of processed foods, fried foods, and fast foods. Aim for an intake of four to five servings of vegetables per day and three to four servings of fruit. Concentrate on whole grains as a staple of your diet, eating three to five servings a day. Healthy fats and good oils (like those that come from olive oil and avocado, plus nuts and seeds) should be consumed five to seven times a day and you should also get one to two servings of beans and legumes. In terms of protein, focus on lean protein options like fish and seafood, aiming for two to six servings per week. Soy foods, Asian mushrooms, herbs, spices, and tea are also important parts of the anti-inflammatory diet. You can also enjoy natural cheeses, yogurt, eggs, and lean meats up to twice a week.

Now that you know the basics about the anti-inflammatory diet you may be eager to get started. This book is just what you need to jump-start your anti-inflammatory diet so you can start to feel better. This book is intended for anyone who would like to give the anti-inflammatory diet a try, but it will be particularly beneficial for those suffering from some type of inflammatory condition. Within this cookbook you will find a wonderful collection of many tasty recipes for breakfast. These recipes are made from fresh, wholesome ingredients including the staples of the anti-inflammatory diet as well as some alkaline-boosting ingredients as well. As an added bonus, many of the recipes in this book are also Paleo- and vegan-friendly.

If you are ready to get started on the anti-inflammatory diet, simply select a recipe and get to cooking!

This book is designed as a simple and practical recipe book. If you wish to learn more about anti-inflammatory diet concepts, check out my book: "Anti-Inflammatory Diet: The Holistic Approach".

Book Link: http://bit.ly/ai-diet-holistic-approach

PART I

Anti-Inflammatory Smoothies

Cucumber Kiwi Green Smoothie

Servings: 1 to 2

Ingredients:

- 2 ripe kiwi fruit
- 1 cup seedless cucumber, chopped
- 1 cup coconut water
- 6 to 8 ice cubes
- ice cubes

- ¼ cup canned coconut milk
- 2 tablespoons fresh chopped cilantro

Instructions:

1. Combine the smoothie ingredients in your high-speed blender.
2. Pulse the ingredients a few times to chop them up.
3. Blend the mixture on the highest speed setting for 30 to 60 seconds.
4. Pour your finished smoothie into glasses and drink.

Tropical Pineapple Kiwi Smoothie

Servings: 1 to 2

Ingredients:

- 1 ½ cups of frozen pineapple
- 1 ripe kiwi, peeled and chopped
- 1 cup of canned full-fat coconut milk
- 6 to 8 ice cubes
- 1 teaspoon spirulina powder
- 3 teaspoons of lime juice

Instructions:

1. Combine the smoothie ingredients in your high-speed blender.
2. Pulse the ingredients a few times to chop them up.
3. Blend the mixture on the highest speed setting.
4. Pour your finished smoothie into glasses and drink.

Sweet Cherry and Chia Smoothie

Servings: 1 to 2

Ingredients:

- 1 ½ cups of frozen or fresh cherries
- 1 small frozen banana
- 1 cup of almond milk
- 6 to 8 ice cubes
- 2 tablespoons of raw chia seeds
- Pinch ground ginger

Instructions:

1. Combine the smoothie ingredients in your high-speed blender.
2. Pulse the ingredients a few times to chop them up.
3. Blend the mixture on the highest speed setting for 30 to 60 seconds.
4. Pour your finished smoothie into glasses and drink.

Spinach Green Tea Smoothie

Servings: 1 to 2

Ingredients:

- 2 cups chopped baby spinach
- 1 medium frozen banana
- 1 small ripe avocado
- 1 ½ cups brewed green tea, chilled

- 2 teaspoons raw honey

Instructions:

1. Combine the smoothie ingredients in your high-speed blender.
2. Pulse the ingredients a few times to chop them up.
3. Blend the mixture on the highest speed setting for 30 to 60 seconds.
4. Pour your finished smoothie into glasses and drink.

Fruity and Spicy Smoothie

Servings: 1 to 2

Ingredients:

- 1 cup frozen or fresh blueberries
- 1 cup frozen or fresh papaya, chopped
- 1 medium frozen banana
- 6 to 8 ice cubes
- 1 ½ cups brewed green tea, chilled
- ¾ teaspoon ground turmeric
- ½ teaspoon ground ginger
- ½ teaspoon ground ginger
- Pinch cayenne pepper
- 4 to 6 drops liquid stevia

Instructions:

1. Combine the smoothie ingredients in your high-speed blender.
2. Pulse the ingredients a few times to chop them up.

3. Blend the mixture on the highest speed setting for 30 to 60 seconds.
4. Pour your finished smoothie into glasses and drink.

Leafy Green Apple Smoothie for Optimal Health

Servings: 1 to 2

Ingredients:

- 2 cups of chopped kale
- 1 medium apple, cored and chopped
- 1 stalk of celery, chopped
- ¼ cup of fresh parsley, minced
- 1 cup of apple juice, unsweetened
- 8 to 10 ice cubes
- 1 tablespoon hemp seeds

Instructions:

1. Combine the smoothie ingredients in your high-speed blender.
2. Pulse the ingredients a few times to chop them up.
3. Blend the mixture on the highest speed setting for 30 to 60 seconds.
4. Pour your finished smoothie into glasses and drink.

Alkalizing Avocado Coconut Smoothie

Servings: 1 to 2

Ingredients:

- 2 cups fresh chopped baby spinach
- 1 small chopped avocado
- ¼ cup of fresh chopped cilantro
- 1 cup chilled coconut water
- 1 tablespoon grated ginger, fresh
- ½ teaspoon ground turmeric
- Pinch cayenne

Instructions:

1. Combine the smoothie ingredients in your high-speed blender.
2. Pulse the ingredients a few times to chop them up.
3. Blend the mixture on the highest speed setting for 30 to 60 seconds.
4. Pour your finished smoothie into glasses and drink.

Blueberry Watermelon Smoothie

Servings: 1 to 2

Ingredients:

- 1 ½ cups frozen blueberries
- 1 ½ cups fresh chopped watermelon
- 1 small ripe banana
- 1-inch fresh sliced ginger
- 1 cup coconut water

- 6 to 8 ice cubes
- 1 tablespoon raw chia seeds

Instructions:

1. Combine the smoothie ingredients in your high-speed blender.
2. Pulse the ingredients a few times to chop them up.
3. Blend the mixture on the highest speed setting for 30 to 60 seconds.
4. Pour your finished smoothie into glasses and drink.

Ginger Berry Green Smoothie

Servings: 1 to 2

Ingredients:

- 2 cups of chopped kale
- 1 ½ cups frozen mixed berries
- 1 medium stalk celery, diced
- 1-inch fresh grated ginger
- 1 cup chilled coconut water
- 1 scoop hemp protein powder

Instructions:

1. Combine the smoothie ingredients in your high-speed blender.
2. Pulse the ingredients a few times to chop them up.
3. Blend the mixture on the highest speed setting for 30 to 60 seconds.
4. Pour your finished smoothie into glasses and drink.

Banana, Honey and Ginger Smoothie

Servings: 1 to 2

Ingredients:

- 1 large frozen banana
- 1 cup chilled almond milk
- ¼ cup of canned coconut milk
- 3 teaspoons honey
- 1 teaspoon grated ginger

Instructions:

1. Combine the smoothie ingredients in your high-speed blender.
2. Pulse the ingredients a few times to chop them up.
3. Blend the mixture on the highest speed setting for 30 to 60 seconds.
4. Pour your finished smoothie into glasses and drink.

Dreamy Yummy Orange Cream Smoothie

Servings: 1 to 2

Ingredients:

- 1 navel orange, peel removed
- 1 cup of almond milk
- 6 to 8 ice cubes
- ½ cup canned full-fat coconut milk
- ¼ cup of fresh orange juice

Instructions:

1. Combine the smoothie ingredients in your high-speed blender.
2. Pulse the ingredients a few times to chop them up.
3. Blend the mixture on the highest speed setting for 30 to 60 seconds.
4. Pour your finished smoothie into glasses and drink.

Blueberry Green Tea Smoothie

Servings: 1 to 2

Ingredients:

- 2 cups frozen or fresh blueberries
- 1 small frozen banana
- 1 cup brewed green tea, chilled
- 6 to 8 ice cubes
- ½ cup of almond milk
- 3 teaspoons of honey

Instructions:

1. Combine the smoothie ingredients in your high-speed blender.
2. Pulse the ingredients a few times to chop them up.
3. Blend the mixture on the highest speed setting for 30 to 60 seconds.
4. Pour your finished smoothie into glasses and drink.

Peachy Keen Smoothie

Servings: 1 to 2

Ingredients:

- 1 ½ cups of frozen peaches
- 1 small frozen banana
- 1 cup of almond milk
- 6 to 8 ice cubes
- 2 tablespoons raw hemp seeds

- Pinch ground ginger

Instructions:

1. Combine the smoothie ingredients in your high-speed blender.
2. Pulse the ingredients a few times to chop them up.
3. Blend the mixture on the highest speed setting for 30 to 60 seconds.
4. Pour your finished smoothie into glasses and drink.

Alkalizing Mango Apricot Smoothie

Servings: 1 to 2

Ingredients:

- 2 cups frozen chopped mango
- 1 cup sliced apricot
- 1 cup unsweetened almond milk
- 6 to 8 ice cubes
- 3 teaspoons fresh lemon juice

Instructions:

1. Combine the smoothie ingredients in your high-speed blender.
2. Pulse the ingredients a few times to chop them up.
3. Blend the mixture on the highest speed setting for 30 to 60 seconds.
4. Pour your finished smoothie into glasses and drink.

Cucumber Melon Smoothie

Servings: 1 to 2

Ingredients:

- 1 ½ cups of chopped honeydew
- 1 cup seedless cucumber, diced
- 1 cup chilled coconut water
- 6 to 8 ice cubes
- 2 tablespoons of fresh mint

Instructions:

1. Combine the smoothie ingredients in your high-speed blender.
2. Pulse the ingredients a few times to chop them up.
3. Blend the mixture on the highest speed setting for 30 to 60 seconds.
4. Pour your finished smoothie into glasses and drink.

Triple Berry Vanilla Smoothie

Servings: 1 to 2

Ingredients:

- 1 cup frozen or fresh strawberries
- ½ cup frozen or fresh blueberries
- ½ cup frozen or fresh blackberries
- 1 cup of vanilla almond milk
- 6 to 8 ice cubes
- 1 tablespoon raw chia seeds
- ½ teaspoon pure vanilla extract

Instructions:

1. Combine the smoothie ingredients in your high-speed blender.
2. Pulse the ingredients a few times to chop them up.
3. Blend the mixture on the highest speed setting for 30 to 60 seconds.
4. Pour your finished smoothie into glasses and drink.

Tropical Mango Coconut Smoothie

Servings: 1 to 2

Ingredients:

- 1 ½ cups of frozen mango
- 1 medium frozen banana
- ½ cup of fresh orange juice
- ½ cup canned coconut milk
- 1 tablespoon of fresh lemon juice

- 1 ½ teaspoons of honey

Instructions:

1. Combine the smoothie ingredients in your high-speed blender.
2. Pulse the ingredients a few times to chop them up.
3. Blend the mixture on the highest speed setting for 30 to 60 seconds.
4. Pour your finished smoothie into glasses and drink.

Blueberry Pomegranate Smoothie

Servings: 1 to 2

Ingredients:

- 2 cups of frozen blueberries
- 1 cup pomegranate juice, unsweetened
- 6 to 8 ice cubes
- ¼ cup of canned coconut milk
- 1 tablespoon hemp seeds

Instructions:

1. Combine the smoothie ingredients in your high-speed blender.
2. Pulse the ingredients a few times to chop them up.
3. Blend the mixture on the highest speed setting for 30 to 60 seconds.
4. Pour your finished smoothie into glasses and drink.

Pineapple and Greens Smoothie

Servings: 1 to 2

Ingredients:

- 1 cup of chopped spinach
- 1 cup of frozen pineapple
- 1 small frozen banana
- ¾ cups of almond milk
- 2 tablespoons chia seeds
- 1 tablespoon of honey

Instructions:

1. Combine the smoothie ingredients in your high-speed blender.
2. Pulse the ingredients a few times to chop them up.
3. Blend the mixture on the highest speed setting for 30 to 60 seconds.
4. Pour your finished smoothie into glasses and drink.

PART II

Energy-Boosting Breakfast Recipes

Mushroom, Spinach and Onion Frittata

Servings: 6

Ingredients:

- 10 large eggs, whisked well
- ½ cup unsweetened almond milk
- Salt and pepper to taste
- 1 tablespoon of coconut oil
- 1 cup diced mushrooms

- 1 small white onion, chopped
- 2 cups fresh chopped spinach

Instructions:

1. Preheat your oven to a temperature of 350°F.
2. Beat together the eggs and almond milk in a small mixing bowl – season the mixture as needed with salt and pepper.
3. Heat the oil in an oven-proof skillet (medium heat)
4. Add the chopped mushrooms. Then, add the onion and then cook for 4 to 5 minutes (until the liquid from the mushrooms has cooked off).
5. Stir in the spinach and cook for another 3 to 4 minutes until wilted.
6. Pour in the egg mixture and cook for about 4 minutes so the bottom starts to set.
7. Transfer your skillet to the oven and bake the frittata for 12 to 15 minutes until set.
8. Cool the frittata for 5 to 10 minutes before slicing.

Sausage and Onion Omelet

Servings: 1

Ingredients:

- 2 teaspoons olive oil, divided
- ½ cup uncooked sausage, crumbled
- ¼ cup diced yellow onion
- 1 teaspoon minced garlic
- 2 large eggs, whisked
- 1 green onion, sliced thin
- 1 tablespoon fresh chopped parsley
- Salt and pepper to taste

Instructions:

1. Heat 1 teaspoon oil in a small nonstick skillet on the medium heat setting.
2. Add the sausage, onions and garlic– cook for a few minutes (until the sausage is nicely browned).
3. Spoon the vegetables off into a bowl and reheat the skillet with the remaining oil.

4. Whisk together the eggs, green onion, salt and pepper.
5. Pour the egg mixture into the skillet and cook for 2 minutes.
6. Loosen the cooked egg around the edges, allowing the uncooked egg to spread.
7. Cook for another 1 to 2 minutes until the egg is almost set.
8. Spoon the sausage and onion mixture over half the omelet.
9. Fold the empty half of the omelet over top.
10. Cook for 1 minute or so more until the egg is set then slide the omelet onto a plate to serve.

Coconut Flour Zucchini Muffins

Servings: 12

Ingredients:

- ¾ cups sifted coconut flour
- 1 teaspoon of baking soda
- 1¼ teaspoon ground cinnamon
- ½ teaspoon ground nutmeg
- 6 large eggs, beaten well

- 1/3 to ½ cup raw honey
- ¼ cup of coconut oil, melted
- 1 teaspoon of pure vanilla extract
- 1½ cups grated zucchini, squeezed to remove moisture

Instructions:

1. Preheat your oven to a temperature of 350°F and line a 12-cup muffin pan with paper muffin wrappers.
2. Whisk together the coconut flour, baking soda, cinnamon and nutmeg in a mixing bowl.
3. In a separate mixing bowl, whisk together the eggs and honey with the coconut oil. Add vanilla extract.
4. Whisk the dry ingredients, stirring until smooth.
5. Fold in the zucchini then spoon the batter into the muffin tin, making sure to fill the cups about ¾ full.
6. Bake for 25 to 30 minutes or until a toothpick comes out clean when pushed into the center.
7. Cool the muffins in the pan for about 5 minutes or so and then turn the muffins out onto a wire rack to cool completely.

Skillet Eggs with Spinach

Servings: 4

Ingredients:

- 1 tablespoon olive oil
- 1 medium yellow onion, chopped
- 10 to 12 cups fresh chopped spinach
- 1 teaspoon fresh lemon juice
- Salt and pepper to taste
- 4 large eggs

Instructions:

1. Preheat your oven to a temperature of 300°F.
2. Heat your oil in a large oven-proof skillet on the medium heat setting.
3. Stir in the onion and cook for a few minutes, until softened.
4. Stir in the spinach and lemon juice then season with salt and pepper.
5. Cook for 4 to 5 minutes until the spinach is wilted.

6. Spread the spinach evenly in the skillet and make four depressions in it.
7. Crack an egg into each hole in the spinach and season it as needed with salt and pepper as needed.
8. Transfer the skillet to the oven and then let it bake for 12 to 15 minutes.

Eggs Baked in Avocado

Servings: 6 to 8

Ingredients:

- 4 medium ripe avocadoes
- 8 large eggs
- Salt and pepper to taste

Instructions:

1. Preheat your oven to a temperature of 425°F.
2. Cut the avocadoes in half and remove the pit – scoop out 2 to 3 tablespoons of avocado from the middle of each half.
3. Place the halves cut-side up in a glass baking dish.
4. Crack an egg into each of the avocado halves and season as needed with salt and pepper.
5. Bake for 16 to 20 minutes until the egg is set. Serve hot.

Herbed Onion Omelet

Servings: 1

Ingredients:

- 2 teaspoons olive oil, divided
- ¼ cup diced yellow onion
- 1 teaspoon minced garlic
- 2 large eggs, beaten
- 1 green onion, sliced thin
- 1 tablespoon of fresh chopped parsley
- Salt and pepper to taste
- 2 tablespoons of fresh chopped cilantro
- 1 tablespoon of fresh chopped basil
- 1 tablespoon of fresh chopped mint

Instructions:

1. Heat 1 teaspoon oil in a small nonstick skillet over medium heat.
2. Add the onions and garlic– cook for 4 to 6 minutes until tender.

3. Spoon the vegetables off into a bowl and reheat the skillet with the remaining oil.
4. Whisk together the eggs, green onion, parsley, salt and pepper.
5. Pour the egg mixture into the skillet and cook for 2 minutes.
6. Loosen the cooked egg around the edges, allowing the uncooked egg to spread.
7. Cook for another 1 to 2 minutes until the egg is almost set.
8. Spoon the onion mixture over half the omelet and sprinkle with herbs.
9. Fold the empty half of the omelet over top.
10. Cook for 1 minute or so more until the egg is set then slide the omelet onto a plate to serve.

Greek-Style Spinach Frittata

Servings: 6

Ingredients:

- 10 large eggs, beaten well
- ½ cup unsweetened almond milk
- 2 scallions, sliced thin
- ½ cup sliced black olives
- ¼ teaspoon dried thyme
- ¼ teaspoon dried rosemary
- Salt and pepper to taste
- 1 tablespoon coconut oil
- ½ small red onion, chopped
- 1 tablespoon minced garlic
- 2 cups fresh chopped spinach

Instructions:

1. Preheat your oven to a temperature of 350°F.

2. Beat together your eggs and the almond milk with the olives and scallions in a small mixing bowl – season the mixture with the thyme, rosemary, salt and pepper to taste.
3. Heat the oil in an oven-proof skillet over medium heat
4. Add the onion and garlic then cook for 4 to 5 minutes until the liquid from the mushrooms has cooked off.
5. Stir in the spinach and cook for 3 to 4 minutes until wilted.
6. Pour in the egg mixture and cook for 4 minutes until the bottom starts to set.
7. Transfer the skillet to the oven and bake for 12 to 15 minutes until the egg is set.
8. Cool the frittata for 5 to 10 minutes before slicing. Garnish with fresh parsley.

Apple Cinnamon Muffins

Servings: 12

Ingredients:

- ¾ cups sifted coconut flour
- 1 teaspoon of baking soda
- 1 ½ teaspoons ground cinnamon
- 6 large eggs, beaten well
- ½ cup unsweetened applesauce

- ¼ cup raw honey
- 1 teaspoon vanilla extract
- 1 medium ripe apple, peeled and chopped

Instructions:

1. Preheat your oven to a temperature of 350°F and line a muffin pan with paper liners.
2. Whisk together the baking soda and coconut flour with the cinnamon in a medium mixing bowl.
3. In a separate mixing bowl, beat together your eggs and honey with the applesauce and pure vanilla extract.
4. Whisk the dry ingredients into the wet, stirring until smooth.
5. Fold in the chopped apple then spoon the muffin batter into the muffin tin, filling each cup about ¾ full.
6. Bake for 25 to 30 minutes until a toothpick pushed into the center comes out clean.
7. Cool the muffins in the pan for 5 minutes then turn out onto a wire rack to cool completely.

Onion Ring Baked Eggs

Servings: 6

Ingredients:

- 2 medium onions, cut into thick slices
- 6 large eggs
- Salt and pepper to taste

Instructions:

1. Preheat your oven to a temperature of 400°F.
2. Divide the slices of onion into rings several layers thick.
3. Heat the oil in an oven-proof skillet on the medium-high heat setting.
4. Place 6 onion rings into the skillet and cook until the edges are caramelized.
5. Crack an egg into each onion ring and cook for about 2 minutes.
6. Season as needed with salt and pepper and then transfer your skillet to the preheated oven.
7. Bake for 12 to 15 minutes until the eggs are cooked to the desired level. Serve hot.

Spicy Sausage and Onion Frittata

Servings: 6

Ingredients:

- 10 large eggs, beaten well
- ½ cup unsweetened almond milk
- 2 serrano peppers, cored and diced
- Salt and pepper to taste
- 1 tablespoon coconut oil

- 1 small white onion, chopped
- 1 teaspoon minced garlic
- ½ lbs. spicy Italian sausage, crumbled

Instructions:

1. Preheat your oven to a temperature of 350°F.
2. Beat together your eggs, almond milk and serrano peppers in a small bowl – season as needed with salt and pepper.
3. Heat the oil in an oven-proof skillet on the medium heat setting.
4. Add the chopped onion and the garlic. Cook for a few minutes (until translucent).
5. Stir in the sausage and cook until evenly browned – drain the fat.
6. Pour in the egg mixture and cook for 4 minutes until the bottom starts to set.
7. Transfer the skillet to the oven and bake for 12 to 15 minutes until the egg is set.
8. Cool the frittata for 5 to 10 minutes before slicing.

Paleo Blueberry Cinnamon Muffins

Servings: 12

Ingredients:

- 2 ½ cups blanched almond flour
- 2 tablespoons sifted coconut flour
- ¾ teaspoon baking soda
- ½ teaspoon ground cinnamon
- ¼ teaspoon salt
- ¼ cup raw honey
- ¼ cup coconut oil, melted
- ¼ cup canned coconut milk
- 2 large eggs, beaten well
- 1 ½ cups fresh blueberries

Instructions:

1. Preheat your oven to a temperature of 350°F and line a muffin pan with paper liners.
2. Whisk together the flours with the baking soda, cinnamon and salt in a medium mixing bowl.

3. In another mixing bowl, whisk together your eggs and honey with the coconut oil, and coconut milk.
4. Whisk the dry ingredients into the wet, stirring until smooth.
5. Fold in the blueberries.
6. Spoon the batter into the prepared tin, filling the cups about ¾ full.
7. Bake for 25 to 30 minutes.
8. Cool the muffins in the pan for 5 minutes then turn out onto a wire rack to cool completely.

Mushroom and Onion Omelet

Servings: 1

Ingredients:

- 2 teaspoons olive oil, divided
- ½ cup diced mushrooms
- ¼ cup diced yellow onion
- 2 large eggs, beaten
- 1 green onion, sliced thin

- Salt and pepper to taste

Instructions:

1. Heat 1 teaspoon oil in a small nonstick skillet over medium heat.
2. Add the mushrooms and onions – cook for 4 to 6 minutes until tender.
3. Spoon the vegetables off into a bowl and reheat the skillet with the remaining oil.
4. Whisk together the eggs, green onion, salt and pepper.
5. Pour the egg mixture into the skillet and cook for 2 minutes.
6. Loosen the cooked egg around the edges, allowing the uncooked egg to spread.
7. Cook for another 1 to 2 minutes until the egg is almost set.
8. Spoon the cooked mushrooms and onions over half the omelet and then fold the empty half over.
9. Cook for 1 minute or so more until the egg is set then slide the omelet onto a plate to serve.

Paleo Spiced Pumpkin Muffins

Servings: 12

Ingredients:

- ½ cup sifted coconut flour
- 1 teaspoon of baking powder
- 1 teaspoon of baking soda
- 1teaspoon ground cinnamon
- ½ teaspoon ground nutmeg
- ¼ teaspoon ground cloves
- Pinch salt
- 6 large eggs, beaten well
- 2/3 cup pumpkin puree
- 2/3 cup raw honey
- ½ cup of coconut oil, melted
- 1 ½ teaspoons of pure vanilla extract

Instructions:

1. Preheat your oven to a temperature of 350°F and line a 12-cup muffin pan with liners.

2. Whisk together the baking soda and coconut flour with the baking powder, cinnamon, nutmeg, cloves and salt in a medium mixing bowl.
3. In a separate bowl, beat together your pumpkin and eggs with the honey, coconut oil, and vanilla extract.
4. Whisk the dry ingredients into the wet, stirring until smooth.
5. Spoon the muffin batter into the muffin tin, filling each cup about ¾ full.
6. Bake for 35 to 40 minutes. Make sure a knife comes out clean when inserted in the center.
7. Cool the muffins in the pan for 5 minutes then turn out onto a wire rack to cool completely.

PART III

Easy Breakfast Wraps and Crepes

Gluten-Free Matcha Crepes

Servings: 10 to 12

Ingredients:

- 1 ¼ cups gluten-free flour blend
- 1 to 2 teaspoons matcha powder
- 2 large eggs, beaten well
- 1 cup of almond milk
- 2 tablespoons of coconut oil, melted
- 1 ½ tablespoons of honey

- 1 teaspoon of pure vanilla extract

Instructions:

1. Combine all of the ingredients together inside a high-speed blender.
2. Blend the mixture on the high speed setting until smooth.
3. Heat a small non-stick skillet on the low heat setting and spray with cooking spray.
4. Pour in about ¼ cup of batter and tilt the pan to evenly coat the bottom.
5. Cook for 1 to 2 minutes until the edges of the crepe are dry and browned.
6. Carefully loosen the edges of the crepe and flip it in a single movement.
7. Cook for another 1 minute or so until the crepe is fully cooked and then transfer them to a plate to keep warm.
8. Repeat the process using the rest of the batter then fill your crepes as desired.

Paleo-Friendly Coconut Wraps

Servings: 6

Ingredients:

- ½ cup arrowroot powder
- ½ tablespoon coconut flour
- Pinch salt
- 4 large eggs, beaten well
- 2 tablespoons warm water
- 2 teaspoons coconut oil, melted

Instructions:

1. Beat together the eggs, water, and coconut oil in a bowl until they are well combined.
2. Whisk in the arrowroot powder, coconut flour and salt.
3. Heat a small skillet on the medium heat setting.
4. Add about 1/3 cup of your wrap batter and tilt the pan to coat the skillet bottom.
5. Cook for 1 minute until the edges of the wrap begin to peel away from the pan.

6. Flip the wrap and cook for about 1 minute more on the other side.
7. Cool the wraps to room temperature and store in a zippered plastic bag.

Homemade Brown Rice Wraps

Servings: 9 to 10

Ingredients:

- 2 ¼ cups brown rice flour
- ¾ cups tapioca flour
- ¾ teaspoon salt
- 1 ½ cups boiling hot water
- Olive oil, as needed

Instructions:

1. Whisk together your three dry ingredients in a mixing bowl until they are well combined.
2. Add the water and knead the mixture into a dough – add the water 1 tablespoon at a time as needed.
3. Let the dough rest for several minutes while you preheat a 10-inch cast-iron skillet over medium heat.
4. Divide the dough by hand into nine or ten even-sized balls by hand.
5. Roll the dough balls out between two pieces of waxed paper into thin circles.

6. Add 1 teaspoon of oil to the skillet and add one of the dough circles.
7. Cook for 1 to 2 minutes then flip the tortilla and cook for another 1 to 2minutes until lightly browned.
8. Transfer the tortilla to a plate to keep warm and repeat with the remaining batter.
9. Wrap the tortillas in a clean towel and let rest for 15 to 20 minutes until soft.

Avocado Egg Salad Breakfast Wrap

Servings: 4 to 6

Ingredients:

- 4 hardboiled eggs, peeled and diced
- 1 medium ripe avocado, pitted and chopped
- 1 ½ to 2 of tablespoons vegan mayonnaise substitute
- 1 ¼ teaspoon curry powder
- Salt and pepper to taste

- 4 to 6 prepared wraps

Instructions:

1. Place the hardboiled eggs and avocado in a mixing bowl.
2. Mash the mixture gently with a fork.
3. Stir in the vegan mayonnaise substitute along with the curry powder.
4. Season the mixture as needed with salt and pepper.
5. Spoon about 1 cup of the mixture down the center of a wrap.
6. Roll the wrap up around the filling and cut in half at an angle to serve.

Onion, Egg and Spinach Breakfast Wrap

Servings: 4

Ingredients:

- 1 teaspoon of olive oil
- 6 ounces' fresh spinach, chopped
- 5 large eggs plus 2 whites, beaten
- Salt and pepper to taste
- 4 prepared wraps
- 1 small ripe avocado, pitted and sliced thin

Instructions:

1. Heat the oil in a small skillet on the medium-high heat setting.
2. Add the spinach and cook for 2 minutes or until just wilted.
3. Beat together the eggs and egg whites in a bowl.
4. Pour the eggs into the skillet and season as needed with salt and pepper.
5. Cook for about 3 to 4 minutes, while stirring occasionally, or until your eggs are set.

6. Spoon about ¼ of the spinach and egg mixture into each tortilla.
7. Top the egg mixture with slices of avocado and roll the wraps up around the filling.

Egg, Ham and Onion Breakfast Wrap

Servings: 4

Ingredients:

- 2 teaspoons olive oil
- 4 large eggs, beaten
- Salt and pepper to taste
- ½ cup diced ham
- ½ small yellow onion, chopped
- 4 prepared wraps

Instructions:

1. Heat your olive oil in a medium non-stick skillet on the medium heat setting.
2. Bea the eggs with some salt and pepper and then pour the eggs into the skillet.
3. Cook the eggs for 2 minutes without disturbing then stir.
4. Allow the eggs to cook for another 1 to 2 minutes, stirring often, until almost set.
5. Stir in the onion and diced ham.

6. Cook for 2 to 3 minutes, stirring often, until the ham is heated through.
7. Spoon about ¼ of the egg and ham mixture down the middle of each wrap.
8. Roll the wraps up around the filling and cut in half to serve.

Paleo-Friendly Tapioca Flour Crepes

Servings: 4

Ingredients:

- 2 cups tapioca flour
- 2 cups canned coconut milk (full fat)
- 2 large eggs, beaten well
- ½ teaspoon salt

Instructions:

1. Combine all of the ingredients in a high-speed blender.
2. Blend the ingredients together on the high speed setting until they are smooth and well combined
3. Heat a small non-stick skillet on the medium heat setting and spray it lightly with cooking spray.
4. Pour in about 1/3 cup of batter and tilt the pan to evenly coat the bottom.
5. Cook for 2 to 3 minutes until the edges of the crepe are dry and browned.
6. Carefully loosen the edges of the crepe and flip it in a single movement.

7. Cook for another 1 to 2 minutes or so until the crepe is fully cooked then transfer to a plate to keep warm.
8. Repeat the process using the rest of the batter then fill your crepes as desired.

Easy Rice Flour Crepes

Servings: 9 to 10

Ingredients:

- 2 cups fine white rice flour
- 2 cups unsweetened almond milk
- 2 large eggs, beaten well
- ¼ cup olive oil
- Extra oil for cooking

Instructions:

1. Combine the ingredients in a medium mixing bowl and whisk them together until smooth and well combined.
2. Heat 2 teaspoons of oil in a small skillet on the medium heat setting.
3. Once the skillet is very hot, pour in about ¼ cup of the batter and tilt the pan to coat the bottom.
4. Cook for 1 to 2 minutes until the edges of the crepe are dry and browned.
5. Carefully loosen the edges of the crepe and flip it in a single movement.

6. Cook for another 1 to 2 minutes or so until the crepe is fully cooked then transfer to a plate to keep warm.
7. Repeat the process using the rest of the batter then fill your crepes as desired.

Paleo Coconut Flour Crepes

Servings: 10 to 12

Ingredients:

- 1 cup unsweetened almond milk
- 6 large eggs, beaten well
- ½ tablespoon olive oil
- 3 tablespoons sifted coconut flour
- Pinch salt

- Coconut oil for cooking

Instructions:

1. Combine the ingredients in a mixing bowl and whisk until smooth and well combined.
2. Let the batter rest for about 10 minutes to absorb all of the liquid.
3. Heat 1 tablespoon of coconut oil in a small skillet. Use medium-high heat.
4. Once the skillet is very hot, pour in about ¼ cup of the batter and tilt the pan to coat the bottom.
5. Cook for 1 to 2 minutes until the edges of the crepe are dry and browned.
6. Carefully loosen the edges of the crepe and flip it in a single movement.
7. Cook for another 15 to 30 seconds until the crepe is fully cooked then transfer to a plate to keep warm.
8. Repeat the process using the rest of the batter then fill your crepes as desired.

Banana and Hemp Protein Crepes

Servings: 4 to 6

Ingredients:

- 3 cups of almond milk
- 2 tablespoons of coconut oil, melted
- 2 cups fine white rice flour
- ¼ cup hemp seeds (raw)
- 1 ripe banana, peeled and mashed
- Olive oil, as needed

Instructions:

1. Whisk together the almond milk, coconut oil, rice flour, and hemp seeds in a mixing bowl.
2. Stir the mixture until well combined and then fold in the mashed banana – stir until lump-free.
3. Heat 1 to 2 teaspoons of olive oil in a small non-stick skillet on the medium heat setting.
4. Pour in about ¼ cup of the batter and tilt the pan to coat the bottom.

5. Cook for 2 to 3 minutes until the edges of the crepe are dry and browned.
6. Carefully loosen the edges of the crepe and flip it in a single movement.
7. Cook for another 1 to 2 minutes until the crepe is fully cooked then transfer to a plate to keep warm.
8. Repeat the process using the rest of the batter then fill your crepes as desired.

Almond Butter and Banana-Filled Crepes

Servings: 4 to 6

Ingredients:

- ¼ to 1/3 cup natural almond butter
- 2 medium ripe bananas, peeled and sliced
- Raw honey, as needed

Instructions:

1. Prepare your crepes using your preferred recipe.
2. Spoon about 1 tablespoon of almond butter down the center of each crepe.
3. Top the almond butter with slices of banana.
4. Roll the crepes up around the filling and drizzle with honey to serve.

Sweet Cinnamon Apple Crepes

Servings: 4 to 6

Ingredients:

- 1 ½ cups chopped apple
- ¼ cup unsweetened apple juice
- 1 ½ tablespoons coconut oil
- 1 ½ teaspoons ground cinnamon

Instructions:

1. Prepare your crepes using your preferred recipe.
2. Combine the apples, cinnamon, coconut oil and apple juice in a small saucepan.
3. Heat the mixture over medium heat and cook until the apples are tender.
4. Spoon about ¼ cup of the apple mixture down the center of each crepe.
5. Roll the crepes up around the filling and serve warm.

Chocolate Hazelnut Crepes

Servings: 4 to 6

Ingredients:

- 2 cups of raw hazelnuts
- 2 ½ tablespoons of unsweetened cocoa powder
- ½ teaspoon of pure vanilla extract
- 15 to 20 drops liquid stevia

Instructions:

1. Prepare your crepes using your preferred recipe.
2. Preheat your oven to a temperature of 375°F and line a rimmed baking sheet with a piece of parchment.
3. Spread the hazelnuts on the baking sheet and roast for 12 to 15 minutes.
4. Place the roasted nuts into a small metal mixing bowl.
5. Cover the mixing bowl with a second bowl about the same size and then shake vigorously until most of the skins have come off of the hazelnuts.
6. Place the hazelnuts (minus the skins) in your food processor and then pulse into a powder.
7. Blend the hazelnuts until they form a smooth butter, using a spoon to scrape down the sides of the processor bowl.
8. Add the cocoa powder, vanilla extract, and stevia.
9. Blend the mixture until smooth then spoon a few tablespoons down the center of each crepe.
10. Roll the crepes up around the filling and serve warm.

Pineapple Coconut Crepes

Servings: 4 to 6

Ingredients:

- 1 tablespoon coconut oil
- 2 cups fresh chopped pineapple
- ½ cup unsweetened shredded coconut
- 2 tablespoons coconut butter, melted
- ¼ cup raw chopped walnuts

Instructions:

1. Prepare your crepes using your preferred recipe.
2. Heat the coconut oil in a small saucepan on the medium heat setting.
3. Stir in the pineapple and coconut – cook for 6 to 8 minutes until the pineapple is tender.
4. Remove the saucepan from heat and stir in the coconut butter and walnuts.
5. Spoon about ¼ cup of the pineapple coconut mixture down the center of each crepe.
6. Roll the crepes up around the filling and serve warm.

PART IV

Anti-Inflammatory Bakes and Bowls

Sausage and Egg Breakfast Bake

Servings: 8 to 10

Ingredients:

- 1 lbs. ground pork sausage
- 1 ½ cups diced sweet potato
- 1 medium yellow onion, chopped
- 3 cups fresh chopped spinach
- 12 large eggs, beaten well

- Salt and pepper to taste

Instructions:

1. Preheat your oven to a temperature of 375°F and grease a rectangular baking dish with cooking spray.
2. Cook the sausage in a large skillet on the medium-high heat setting until it is browned.
3. Drain the fat from the sausage then spread it in the baking dish.
4. Reheat the skillet with 1 teaspoon of sausage grease.
5. Add the sweet potatoes and onion.
6. Cook for 6 to 8 minutes until tender.
7. Stir in the spinach and cook for 1 to 2 minutes.
8. Spoon the veggies into your glass baking dish, stirring with the sausage.
9. Beat the eggs with the salt and pepper then pour into the dish.
10. Bake for 25 to 30 minutes until the center is set.
11. Allow the casserole to cool for 10 minutes before serving.

Cinnamon Spiced Quinoa Bowl

Servings: 4

Ingredients:

- 1 cup uncooked quinoa
- 1 ½ cups water
- ½ teaspoon ground cinnamon
- Pinch salt

Instructions:

1. Rinse the quinoa well.
2. Combine the quinoa, water, cinnamon and salt in a medium-sized saucepan.
3. Bring the mixture to a boil.
4. Turn down the heat, cover, and simmer for 15 minutes.
5. When cooked, remove the saucepan from the heat. Cool down.
6. Serve drizzled with coconut milk.

Simply Paleo Porridge

Servings: 1

Ingredients:

- ¼ cup chopped walnuts
- 3 tablespoons shredded coconut, unsweetened
- 2 tablespoons pumpkin seeds
- 1 tablespoon raw chia seeds
- 1 ¼ teaspoon ground cinnamon
- Pinch salt
- 1 cup boiling hot water

Instructions:

1. Combine your ingredients in the bowl of your food processor.
2. Pulse a few times until your mixture has been powdered.
3. Pour in the boiling hot water then blend well until the mixture is very smooth and well combined.
4. Spoon the porridge into a bowl and top with raisins and a drizzle of coconut milk.

Mixed Veggie Baked Quiche

Servings: 8

Ingredients:

- ½ lbs. uncooked pork sausage
- 2 cups blanched almond flour
- 2 tablespoons coconut oil
- ½ teaspoon salt
- 10 large eggs, divided

- 2 tablespoons water
- 1 ½ cups fresh chopped broccoli

Instructions:

1. Preheat your oven to a temperature of 350°F.
2. Heat your olive oil in a skillet on the medium heat setting.
3. Add the mushrooms, onion and carrot – cook for 6 to 8 minutes until tender.
4. Combine the almond flour, coconut oil, and salt with one egg in a food processor.
5. Blend until it forms a sticky dough.
6. Spread the dough in a pie plate or quiche dish, pressing it evenly into the bottom and up the sides.
7. Spoon the cooked veggies into the dish, spreading evenly.
8. Beat together the remaining eggs with the water and pour into the dish.
9. Bake for 30 to 35 minutes until the quiche is set.

Honey Walnut Quinoa Bowl

Servings: 6

Ingredients:

- 1 ½ cups uncooked quinoa
- 2 ½ cups water
- 1 teaspoon ground cinnamon
- Pinch salt
- 1/3 cup chopped walnuts
- Raw honey, as needed

Instructions:

1. Rinse the quinoa well until the water runs clear.
2. Combine the quinoa, water, cinnamon and salt (I recommend you use a medium saucepan).
3. Bring the mixture to a boil.
4. Wait a bit and reduce heat and simmer for about 15 minutes.
5. Once the quinoa has absorbed the water then take it off the heat and let it stand (covered) for 5 minutes.

6. Fluff the cooked quinoa with a fork and then spoon into bowls.
7. Top the quinoa bowls with chopped walnuts and a drizzle of honey.

Amaranth Coconut Porridge

Servings: 4

Ingredients:

- 3 cups water
- 1 cup amaranth
- ¼ teaspoon salt
- 1 cup canned coconut milk
- ½ cup shredded coconut, toasted

Instructions:

1. Take a small saucepan and bring the water to boil,
2. Whisk in the amaranth and salt then reduce heat and simmer, covered, for 20 minutes.
3. Remove the sauce pan from the heat and stir in the coconut milk as well as the toasted coconut.
4. Spoon into bowls and serve topped with chopped nuts, if desired.

Spinach, Mushroom and Sweet Potato Breakfast Bake

Servings: 8 to 10

Ingredients:

- 2 tablespoons coconut oil
- 4 cups diced sweet potato
- 2 cups diced mushrooms
- 1 medium yellow onion, chopped
- 2 cups fresh chopped spinach
- 12 large eggs, beaten well
- Salt and pepper to taste

Instructions:

1. Preheat your oven to a temperature of 375°F and grease a rectangular glass baking dish.
2. Heat your oil in a large skillet on the medium-high heat setting.
3. Add the sweet potatoes, mushrooms and onion – cook for about 8 to 10 minutes.

4. Stir in the spinach and cook for 1 to 2 minutes until wilted
5. Spoonthe veggies into the baking dish.
6. Beat the eggs with the salt and pepper then pour into the dish.
7. Bake for 25 to 30 minutes until the center is set.
8. Allow the casserole to cool for 10 minutes before serving.

Cinnamon Pumpkin Porridge

Servings: 4 to 6

Ingredients:

- 2 cups unsweetened almond milk
- 1 ½ cups water
- 1 ½ cup uncooked quinoa
- ¾ cups pumpkin puree
- 1 ½ teaspoons ground cinnamon

- ¼ teaspoon salt
- 3 tablespoons ground flaxseed meal

Instructions:

1. Whisk together the water and almond milk in a medium saucepan.
2. Bring the mixture to boil then stir in the quinoa, pumpkin, cinnamon and salt.
3. Reduce the heat and simmer, covered, for 10 to 12 minutes.
4. Make sure the liquid has been absorbed and move on to the next step.
5. Remove your saucepan from the heat and then stir in your flaxseed meal.
6. Spoon the porridge into small bowls and serve with toasted pumpkin seeds, if desired.

Apple Cinnamon Quinoa Bowl

Servings: 4

Ingredients:

- 1 cup uncooked quinoa
- 1 ½ cups water
- Pinch salt
- 2 medium apples, peeled and chopped
- 1 tablespoon coconut oil
- 1 teaspoon ground cinnamon

Instructions:

1. Rinse the quinoa well until the water runs clear.
2. Combine the quinoa, water, cinnamon and salt in a medium saucepan.
3. Bring the mixture to a boil then reduce heat and simmer, covered, for 20 minutes.
4. Once the quinoa has absorbed the water, remove from heat and cool down.

5. Meanwhile, melt your coconut oil in another saucepan and then stir in the apples and cinnamon.
6. Cook for 8 to 10 minutes on medium heat, stirring occasionally, until the apples are tender.
7. Fluff the quinoa with a fork and spoon into bowls.
8. Spoon the apple mixture on top of the quinoa to serve.

Veggies and Eggs Breakfast Bake

Servings: 8 to 10

Ingredients:

- 2 tablespoons coconut oil
- 2 cups diced mushrooms
- 1 ½ cups diced sweet potato
- 1 cup chopped zucchini
- 1 medium yellow onion, chopped
- 2 cups fresh chopped spinach
- 12 large eggs, beaten well
- 2 green onions, sliced thin
- Salt and pepper to taste

Instructions:

1. Preheat the oven to 375°F and grease a rectangular glass baking dish.
2. Heat your oil in a large skillet on the medium-high heat setting.

3. Add the sweet potatoes, mushrooms, zucchini and onion – cook for 8 to 10 minutes until tender.
4. Stir in the spinach and cook for 1 to 2 minutes until wilted
5. Spoon the veggies into the baking dish.
6. Beat the eggs with the salt and pepper then pour into the dish.
7. Bake for 25 to 30 minutes until the center is set.
8. Allow the casserole to cool for 10 minutes before serving.

Buckwheat and Banana Porridge

Servings: 4

Ingredients:

- 2 cups water
- 2 cups buckwheat grouts
- 4 overripe bananas, peeled and sliced
- 2 tablespoons of honey
- 1 tablespoon ground cinnamon
- 3 to 4 cups of almond milk
- 2 tablespoons natural almond butter

Instructions:

1. Whisk together the water and buckwheat in a medium saucepan.
2. Bring the mixture to boil then stir in the bananas, honey and cinnamon.
3. Cook until the buckwheat absorbs the water then stir in 3 cups of almond milk.

4. Continue cooking the buckwheat, adding up to 1 more cup of almond milk several tablespoons at a time, until very tender.
5. Stir in the almond butter then spoon the porridge into bowls.
6. Serve topped with chopped nuts, if desired.

Broccoli Sausage Baked Quiche

Servings: 8

Ingredients:

- ½ lbs. uncooked pork sausage
- 2 cups blanched almond flour
- 2 tablespoons coconut oil
- ½ teaspoon salt
- 10 large eggs, divided

- 2 tablespoons water
- 1 ½ cups fresh chopped broccoli

Instructions:

1. Preheat your oven to a temperature of 350°F.
2. Cook the sausage in a skillet on the medium-high heat setting until browned – drain the fat and set it aside.
3. Combine the almond flour, coconut oil, and salt with one egg in a food processor.
4. Blend until it forms a sticky dough.
5. Spread the dough in a pie plate or quiche dish, pressing it evenly into the bottom and up the sides.
6. Spoon the sausage into the dish and sprinkle the broccoli over it.
7. Beat together the remaining eggs with the water and pour into the dish.
8. Bake for 30 to 35 minutes until the quiche is set.

Honey Almond Paleo Porridge

Servings: 2

Ingredients:

- ½ cup chopped walnuts
- 1/3 cup shredded coconut, unsweetened
- 3 tablespoons pumpkin seeds
- 2tablespoon chia seeds
- 1 tablespoon ground flaxseed
- 1 teaspoon ground cinnamon
- 1 teaspoon almond extract
- Pinch salt
- 2 cup boiling hot water
- Slivered almonds, to serve
- Raw honey, to serve

Instructions:

1. Combine the ingredients in the bowl of your food processor.
2. Pulse until the mixture has been powdered.

3. Pour in the boiling hot water and then blend until the mixture is smooth.
4. Spoon the porridge into a bowls and top with slivered almonds and a drizzle of honey.

Before you go, I'd like to remind you that there is a free, complimentary eBook waiting for you. Download it today to treat yourself to healthy, gluten-free desserts and snacks so that you never feel deprived again!

Download link:
http://bit.ly/gluten-free-desserts-book

Conclusion

Thank you for reading my book, and thank you for committing to your health. My hope is that you have gained an understanding of how inflammation works in the body and why it is so important to eat in a manner that cools that inflammation, allowing us to feel our best on a daily basis and live disease-free.

The beauty of this diet is that it does not fit into what might be your previous understanding of a *diet*. This is a way of eating that is sustainable for you and your entire family, for a lifetime. The results you will see and feel including sustained energy, decreased mood swings and food sensitivities, increased fitness and so many others, will be the true motivation you need to commit and stay committed.

So... **congratulations!** You have taken an important step. Your body will surely thank you.

If you decide that the anti-inflammatory diet is the lifestyle for you, I hope you will try some of the recipes in this book as you transition into the diet. Please let me know your favorites- the [review section of this book](#) is an excellent place to share your experience with other readers.

To post an honest review

One more thing… If you have received any value from this book, can you please rank it and post a short review? It only takes a few seconds really and it would really make my day. It's you I am writing for and your opinion is always much appreciated. In order to do so;

1. Log into your account
2. Search for my book on Amazon or check your orders / or go to my author page at:

http://amazon.com/author/kira-novac

3. Click on a book you have read, then click on "reviews" and "create your review".

Please let me know your favorite motivational tip you learned from this book.

If you happen to have any questions or doubts about this book, please e-mail me at:

kira.novac@kiraglutenfreerecipes.com

I would love to hear from you!

Recommended Reading

Book Link:

http://bit.ly/af-lunch-recipes

Recommended Reading

Book Link:

http://bit.ly/af-dinner-recipes

FOR MORE HEALTH BOOKS (KINDLE & PAPERBACK) BY KIRA NOVAC PLEASE VISIT:

www.kiraglutenfreerecipes.com/books

Thank you for taking an interest in my work,

Kira and Holistic Wellness Books

HOLISTIC WELLNESS & HEALTH BOOKS

If you are interested in health, wellness, spirituality and personal development, visit our page and be the first one to know about free and 0.99 eBooks:

www.HolisticWellnessBooks.com

www.ingramcontent.com/pod-product-compliance
Lightning Source LLC
Chambersburg PA
CBHW072203100526
44589CB00015B/2352